'In the cool of the day'

creative reflections from the garden

April McIntyre

Foreword

'Perfectly manicured or wild and overgrown,' is how April McIntyre refers to our gardens on the cover of this book.

I am pleased to tell you that what we have here is a wonderful collection of 'perfectly manicured' reflections. The well-crafted prose and elegant poems give a profound sense of the peace and beauty of the garden as a bountiful space where we can reflect upon our lives, our spiritual journeys and observe our Maker at work.

But it is not just the words which speak. I'm a keen proponent of the power of images to complement words and these reflections do this admirably, pulling together verbal and pictorial imagery, in addition to a scripture passage, to lead us by the hand into our own personal time of reflection.

Being close to nature has always been an integral part of our family life, whether we are on our own patch of ground, in a park, on country walks, or wherever we find ourselves outdoors. The therapeutic effect of green space is now well recognized so, in our post-Covid era, this book chimes perfectly with that deeply-felt need to engage with creation.

Our garden at home is just a small plot but it teems with flowers, shrubs and trees. I adore sitting in this small, green space which brings me great peace and solace. So, whether sitting in my own garden or meditating in the virtual world of these reflections, I shall treasure April's collection of words and pictures and hope to deepen my closeness to God.

For, as the poet Dorothy Frances Gurney famously wrote, 'One is nearer God's heart in a garden than anywhere else on earth.'

Richard Palmer, National Groups' Coordinator,
Association of Christian Writers, March 2022.

Contents

Reflections of the Creator are all around us.

Then the man and his wife

heard the sound of the LORD *God*

as he was walking in the garden

in the cool of the day,

and they hid from the LORD *God*

among the trees of the garden.

⁹ But the LORD *God called to the man,*

'Where are you?'

Genesis 3: 8-9

The garden – a place of encounter

Introduction

The end of a long, hot day. Slowly, I connect the hose pipe and begin to work my way around the garden, soaking the dried-out pots; tweaking dead heads, re-filling the bird bath; brushing my hand amongst the rosemary, lavender and thyme. Sometimes, in my enthusiasm, I water my feet by mistake but, on the whole, I am feeling relaxed and close to creation.

It's said that in the very beginning, God would walk around the Garden of Eden looking for Adam and Eve and hoping to enjoy their friendship. In the story, things didn't work out too well but, as I'm pottering about my own garden, with no real agenda – just being in the moment – I often get the feeling that God is walking with me.

What is this God like? A protective, parental figure, arms open wide to give me a hug; a friend I can bounce ideas off or just a delightful whisper of life and creativity? However I see him or her, I believe that this God enjoys our time together in the special stillness that comes *'in the cool of the day'* (Genesis 3:8).

There are many ways that we can spend time with God but, for me, this wandering round the garden really helps. Somehow, my mind eases into neutral. I stop plotting and planning and anxieties begin to dissolve as I respond to what is around me: the smells, the breeze, the colours, the sounds.

I'm sure many people would agree that being out and about in the natural world greatly helps our physical, mental and spiritual well-being.

This truth has been highlighted for us during the Covid-19 lockdowns of 2020 and 2021 which have made us so grateful for the gardens, parks and open spaces that have been our life-line; where we can walk and exercise and find peace as the seasons change around us.

We are living through times when many disasters and conflicts are shaking our world and issues of climate change are forcing us to begin to do things differently. It is my hope that this gentle book of reflections, pictures and poems will encourage us to appreciate the natural world on our doorsteps, to receive its blessings and be ready to protect and care for it. In the process, we may encounter the God who still roams around creation crying, 'Where are you?' I wonder what our response will be.

The reflections in this book loosely follow the changing seasons, from summer through to spring. Read them slowly, thoughtfully, in whatever order seems right to you. Allow them to stimulate your thinking, your prayers and your own creativity as you listen for that 'still, small voice' of the Creator.

Thank you

My thanks to all those who have supported me in my writing over the past few years, especially to my husband, Mike, who is always there for me.

Thanks also to members of the Derby Cathedral Café Writers' Group who have helped me to believe that I have something worth sharing and even worth committing to print. I am particularly grateful to Richard Palmer, leader of Café Writers, for providing such an encouraging foreword to this collection.

Please note that Bible quotations are taken from the New International Version (NIV) unless otherwise stated.
All photographs and drawings are © April McIntyre

Do you have a garden? What does it mean to you?

1. In the garden

Then the man and his wife heard the sound of the Lord God as he was walking in the garden in the cool of the day, and they hid from the Lord God among the trees of the garden. Genesis 3: 8

God walked in the garden
in the cool of the day,
looking for those
he had formed from the clay,
enjoying the goodness
of all he surveyed -
but his friends were avoiding him,
lost and afraid.

Jesus walked in the garden
in the dead of the night,
compelled by compassion
to set all things right.
Imploring his Father,
he fell to his knees -
but his friends were found sleeping,
unaware of his need.

Tears in the garden
in the fresh morning light,
in search of a body
vanished from sight.
Mary's name spoken,
bringing grief to an end –
it was Jesus, alive again,
seeking his friends.

Watering the garden,
as summer sun cools,
there's a whisper, a stirring,
deep in my soul:
creativity, goodness,
life without end -
for it's here, in the stillness,
God calls me his friend.

2. Sad Plants

'I will search for the lost and bring back the strays. I will bind up the injured and strengthen the weak…' Ezekiel 34: 16

God spoke to me in the potting shed one summer's afternoon, as the sparrows chirped lazily in the hedge.

We'd just been down to the DIY store where I'd left my husband browsing round the tools while I sought consolation in the garden centre. I was in luck. They were selling off strips of straggly herbs and vegetables at a bargain price. I love herbs: their versatility, resilience, their wholesome nature. My husband, surveying my purchases, said I just liked rescuing 'sad plants'.

That afternoon, I teased out each plant from the overgrown strips, pruning, removing faded leaves, re-potting, relishing the bruised fragrance of basil, parsley and celery. Time was ticking by but I was enjoying myself. Then, quietly, God spoke. 'What are you doing?' he said. I told him about my sad plants and how I was giving them a new lease of life. I'm sure he knew this already.

'So, you're wasting time on imperfect plants?'
I looked at the rows of bright little pots, seeing so much potential and feeling strangely protective.

'So, can you understand how I feel about <u>my</u> sad plants?' said God. 'And how I feel about you?'

As the sun filtered through the dust and cobwebs on the shed windows, I felt rather warm inside. It struck me that perhaps God enjoys spending time with me even though there are countless people more confident and competent. Maybe I <u>was</u> special to him after all.

I finished the last of the parsley and tidied up in silence. I won't forget this God who comes and reveals his love so simply, in a shed.

Have you ever sensed God speaking through creation?

3. Too hot to move

Whoever dwells in the shelter of the Most High will rest in the shadow of the Almighty. Psalm 91:1

Too hot to move as sunshine blazes
from a picture-postcard sky;
too hot to mow the too-long lawn,
pull-up invading grasses, tackle
wilted weeds. Bees tumble
through the lavender and thyme,
forgetting how to buzz, heavy
legs weary of busyness.
A sentinel sparrow chirps staccato
warnings as washing stiffens on the line.
Suddenly, a great tit darts from cover,
steals a seed and is gone.
Hiding beneath a too-big, floppy
hat and glasses, sheltering within
the umbrella's welcome shade,
I clutch an ice-crammed drink -
too hot to think.
Only the bright, open daisy
flowers gaze gladly heavenwards,
receptive in their worship, as the
sun beats down.
Yet I am grateful for this space,
to be with my Creator God,
until the unrelenting sun
and shrinking shade
move me, slowly, back inside.

Space to be

4. Walking the labyrinth

'Come to me, all you who are weary and burdened, and I will give you rest. Take my yoke upon you and learn from me, for I am gentle and humble in heart and you will find rest for your souls...'
Matthew 11:28-30

The stone was damp on my bare feet as I entered the labyrinth. Breeze, moist earth and birdsong stirred my senses as I walked my prayer in the enclosed garden of the retreat house.

A labyrinth is a walking meditation, a pathway of prayer, an arena where soul meets Spirit. It has only one path that leads from the outer edge to the centre. There are no tricks or dead ends as in a maze and the same path leads out again. Found in many world cultures, these ancient circular patterns have been used through the centuries by those seeking to quiet the mind, open the heart and ground the body.

As I walked, I found that the circular path drew close to the centre of the labyrinth but then quickly veered away into a tangle of intestine-like loops. I began to wonder if I was walking the wrong way altogether.

This is so like our lives. Our paths are never really straight. Who knows what lies around the next bend? We may get excited, thinking we've 'arrived' only to be taken into more twists and challenges. The secret is to relax into a slow rhythm, becoming aware of the movements around and within. Suddenly, you'll find yourself at the centre with time to reflect and be still.

The value of the labyrinth, like any pilgrimage, is not so much journeying to find God as walking with God in the moment. As I slowly placed one foot in front of another, I could imagine Jesus patiently walking with me, urging me to accept his gentle yoke to keep us in step on the journey ahead. What a reassuring message to bring away with me!

None of us, today, know where our paths are taking us, as individuals or as a nation. We may feel uncertain and confused. For Christians, however, what matters most is knowing that, whatever the challenges, Jesus walks at our side. He is *'the way and the truth and the life.' (John 14:6)*

5. The Passion Flower

'Consider how the lilies grow. They do not labour or spin. Yet I tell you, not even Solomon in all his splendour was dressed like one of these.' Luke 12: 27

Are you a sucker for a bargain?

Over the gloomy months of winter I often get bombarded with mail-order plant catalogues, seduced by visions of early flowering bulbs and summer bedding, tempted by special offers and free gifts. I try to resist but the frustrated gardener in me shouts, 'Yes!' That's why, some years ago, I had an uninspiring climber sitting in a pot in a corner of the patio, all leaves and tendrils. It had done nothing for several years and I was ready to throw it out.

Then suddenly, towards the end of summer, it flowered: a spectacular passion flower, blue, purple and white, *passiflora caerulea*. I stared in amazement.

Perhaps the 17th century missionaries who first discovered the plant in South America reacted the same way. They saw, in the unusual flower parts, a reflection of the suffering of Christ on the cross: a central crown of thorns; five stamens representing Christ's wounds; three nail-like stigmas; the curling whip-like tendrils; spear-shaped leaves.

To them it became The Passion Flower, a living icon, a window into God's mystery.

These days, we may feel that the symbolism is a bit exaggerated yet you can't deny the impact of these striking flowers. However busy or absorbed I am, they compel me to stop, to 'stand and stare'.

I catch a whisper that God's self-giving love is no fragile, hot-house bloom but something strong and vigorous, biding its time in quiet corners, scrambling round and through obstacles and suddenly blazing out to delight us.

We all have times when the days are dreary and we feel like giving up yet God's love may still surprise us, radiating hope and transforming our barren places.

The passion flower

6. Making Chutney

Only three more days to go –
or is it four? I peer into the
cupboard to check the dates
on the jars. Soon it will be
time to sample my chutney.

I made it back in
August when the fridge was
heavy with bulging, dark
green produce from the
garden. Courgettes don't
freeze too well and there's only so much ratatouille you can
cope with so I opted for chutney: finely chopping courgettes,
apricots and apples; onions that made me cry; vinegar for
bite; sugar for sweetness, all stirred together in a mighty pan,
permeating the house with eye-watering aromas.

Shopping in large supermarkets, with fruit and
vegetables imported all year round, it's easy to lose track of
the changing seasons so there's something very special
about growing and using your own produce. And what can
be better than cheering up your Christmas pork pie with tasty
home-made chutney? As you eat, it brings back memories of
days in the garden, wind and sunshine on your face, working
hard, sipping an ice-cold drink, tackling the menace of killer
slugs.

That taste of summer does us so much good,
psychologically as well as nutritionally. Wouldn't it be good if
we could bottle the good times so that when days are grey
and wearisome, we could reach for the jar, unscrew the top

and savour the sweetness: exulting in being alive, being truly loved and knowing that touch of God's presence with us.

In times past, such blessings were known as consolations - experiences that are life-enriching, heart-warming, uplifting. Today, people of faith may still take time at the end of the day to reflect on what they are most grateful for, seeking to discern where God is moving in it all.

As autumn colours creep over the landscape and crisp winds chase away summer indolence, perhaps we too should gather together a few consolations, storing them in our hearts and minds to sustain us as darker days close in.

7. Kicking Leaves

'I have come that they may have life, and have it to the full.'
John 10:10

Joy of kicking leaves!
Shuffling,
scrunching,
scuffing frustrations
in the dust.
Heart lifts
as unexpected sunshine
touches russet,
gold and brown
and baby-blue
plays hide and seek
between the clouds.
Summer fashions,
randomly discarded,
now delight.
I stomp and kick
wondering
if anyone will see
the child
peeping shyly
out of me.

How do you express your delight in creation?

8. Picking blackberries

Let us throw off everything that hinders and the sin that so easily entangles, and let us run with perseverance the race marked out for us. Hebrews 12: 1

A thorny branch whipped back as I strained into the heart of the brambles, scoring my arm with pinpricks of blood. Undeterred, I reached further and plucked the fat, juicy blackberries nestling there.

I grew up on the outskirts of Stoke-on-Trent, a few minutes' drive from quiet, country lanes, disused railway tracks and those secret, 'wild' places where our family sought the best berries. On Sundays, towards the end of summer, we would jump in the car with our strange assortment of cans and baskets and set off. We picked in our own ways, sometimes together, sometimes drifting off alone as leaves reddened and the late sunshine glowed on our cheeks. Autumn was on its way and the challenges of a new school year lay ahead.

Some of our blackberries would be stewed or made into pies but most were washed and poured, with apple and sugar, into our huge brass jam kettle. Jamming was my father's job. Over the years he must have produced hundreds of jars, stored in the pantry under the stairs and lasting us throughout the year, with 'bread and jam' supplementing many a scanty meal.

As I grew older, I began to wonder if all that effort - the snagged clothing, stained hands and embedded thorns, the tedious washing of jam jars - was really worth it. Today, indeed, it seems so much easier to buy what we need from the vast array of produce in the supermarkets. Yet, looking back, I realise the value of those family times out in the natural world and how much they added to my life then and now.

Living a life of faith is a bit like picking blackberries. It's certainly not easy! Doubts prick us, troubles lash us and sometimes there is no evidence of fruit at all. Ironically, as in nature, it often seems that the sweetest fruit and most delicate flowers are those growing on the prickliest stems!

Yet, despite the cost, we press on, working together, encouraging one another and realising how much we have to be grateful for. And, through it all, God is with us. His sweet grace continues to nourish and sustain us even as autumn moves on into winter.

What do you feel grateful for today?
Why not thank God now?

9. Pensées

Let us fix our eyes on Jesus…who for the joy set before him endured the cross. Consider him…so that you will not grow weary and lose heart. Hebrews 12: 2-3

Growing up in the Potteries, I was used to the smell of turpentine that pervaded our house; used to the sight of a rickety table set out with brushes, colours, palette knife and half-finished ware; familiar with the sight of my mother laboriously painting ceramic jewellery and flower bowls hour after hour, fitting in her job around family life. I remember watching, fascinated, as she painted the pansies, delicately shading round the edges of the petals, blending the darker blotches, deftly adding the streaks. Perhaps this is why I've always loved pansies.

Cultivated and developed extensively in Victorian times, pansies (from pensées in French) are associated with thoughts and with love. Sown in early autumn, hardy winter varieties will grow and flower as the days shorten, through wind, rain and even snow, splashing their cheer throughout our parks and gardens, faces turned towards the fleeting sun.

What an inspiration! When days are shrouded with autumnal mists and chilly air; when we are wrestling with challenges, uncertain what lies ahead, we can still turn our own faces towards the Son - to the God who loves us, who died for us and who walks with us by his Spirit through summer sunshine and winter storms alike.

And so I think back again to my mother, in the last years of her life, even in the difficult months of chemotherapy. And she was still painting – but now decorating bookmarks and pebbles with little pictures and Bible verses to give away to others. For she too was turning her gaze towards the God she loved so dearly.

10. The Falling

We know that the whole creation has been groaning as in the pains of childbirth right up to the present time. Romans 8: 22

Autumn touches trees with transformation,
recycling waste to please an artist's gaze,
blushing gold and red in dappled sunlight,
bronzing browns and peachy orange haze.
Swirling drifts of dry leaves dance and scatter,
heaping by the berry-burnished hedge;
persistent flowers splash colour in the borders
though heavy-lidded clouds loom overhead.
Morning mists give way to fiery splendour;
breath-smoking stars sprinkle night with awe;
questing squirrels scrabble in the shadows
as bold-eyed robin flaunts his winter coat.
Time for us to chop and prune and tidy,
preparing ground afresh for next year's things,
bending low and risking chronic backache
for bulbs, already dreaming of the spring.
Now's the time to dig out chunky jumpers,
and brave the chill that sharpens darker days,
to snuggle deep beneath a cosy duvet,
warmed by wholesome stews and firelight's blaze.
As smells and signs and symbols stir our spirits
and candles chase the shadows round the room,
we hear the Maker walking in his garden,
gracious footsteps pounding in our blood.
For surely God is faithful in the Falling,
remembering our weaknesses and strife.
He hears the constant groaning of Creation,
dropping hints of resurrection life.

How have you experienced God's faithfulness?

11. Footsteps of his Coming

A voice of one calling: 'In the desert prepare the way for the Lord;
make straight in the wilderness a highway for our God...'
Isaiah 40:3-5

Barren branches,
stretched in supplication
to a sunless sky;
chaos of dying stems,
piercing rotting leaves;
boots darkening with damp.

Behind the chill,
a hush of stillness.

I clutch a scarf around me,
catching covert movements,
hidden in hedges;
surprised
by a single bright,
imperfect rose.

Awaiting,
in this wild place,
the footsteps
of His Coming,
dancing down the glory
of a dying year.

How might we prepare for the coming of the Lord?

12. Amaryllis

Those who hope in the Lord will renew their strength. They will soar on wings like eagles… Isaiah 40:31

It was autumn when I ordered some unusual amaryllis bulbs from a plant catalogue to use as Christmas gifts for friends. I planted four different bulbs and three began to grow almost immediately. By December they had reached a good size with strong stems and sturdy buds.

Meanwhile, the fourth bulb sat in its pot and did nothing. Weeks went by. No sign of growth. Anxiously, I checked the soil and poked around with my finger. Still nothing. Should I throw it away? Write to the bulb company? I waited. Then, in mid-January, when the other amaryllis flowers had bloomed and faded, a green tip appeared. That new shoot seemed to leap upwards in its eagerness to grow.

Well, this got me thinking because, so often, our lives seem just like this. We look at those around us and see so much growth and such impressive achievements but when we look at ourselves, nothing seems to be happening. Perhaps we feel buried in darkness, hurting or afraid.

Throughout the centuries, people of faith have cried out in times of distress, 'How long must we wait? Where is God? Has he heard? Does he care?'

If you feel anything like this in the dark, winter months, let my amaryllis give you hope because God <u>does</u> care. The stories of the birth of Jesus demonstrate how God came in the flesh to live amongst us. He is a God for life not just for Christmas and he is listening to the cries of our hearts.

Even now, things may be stirring deep down in hidden places. We can anxiously prod our circumstances and curse the inactivity or we can pour out our concerns to the God who loves us, the God who is with us, even when we can't see or hear him. So let's wait and trust – and watch for that first glimpse of green.

God does care!

13. Walking slowly through mud

The Lord God formed the man from the dust of the ground and breathed into his nostrils the breath of life, and the man became a living being. Genesis 2: 7

Walking
slowly
through mud:
path pocked,
cow-printed,
liquefying
into treacle puddles.

Walking
slowly,
gingerly,
boots clay-heavy,
sloshing un-carefully
like the child
that never was.

Time to bathe
in sudden sunbursts,
blood-bright holly
splashed along the way.
Breaking silence
with a snatch
of half-forgotten song.

Walking
slowly,
through mud,
solitude is welcome
yet I know I'm not alone,

companioned by one
who nurtures seeds of creativity
in clay.

Where are we going?

We're walking
slowly,
gently,
together
through mud,
until the time
when all mud
is washed away.

14. Choose Life!

I have set before you life and death, blessings and curses. Now choose life, so that you and your children may live and that you may love the Lord your God, listen to his voice, and hold fast to him. Deuteronomy 30: 19-20

I'm feeling rather 'down' today. Outside it is gloomy with a hint of sleet in the driving rain. Bundled into my layers of jumpers and cardigans, I feel cold. It is February.

I've been trying to get some work done but so far have little to show for it. Now it is time for my prayers but I feel heavy, with nothing much to say to God. In the past, I would have prayed around my dark feelings but so often this just makes things worse, dragging me further into a negative, introspective soup.

Instead I play a familiar CD: something quiet, with words rich in wisdom and poignant instrumental voices interweaving. Then I set out my pastels and begin to draw.

I'm not drawing a picture, not trying to produce a work of art – just making shapes and patterns on the paper. I love swirling and mixing the colours, smearing soft pastels with my fingers. It's very messy but satisfying. It bypasses the need for words and seems to unlock something inside me.

I let the music and the movements of my hands work together, not thinking or praying but giving God space. When I've finished, I may have something interesting or just a mess to throw in the bin. That doesn't matter but often something will emerge from the quiet time: a sense of connection with the Creator; a recognition of myself as God's child; an uplift of energy and new ideas.

In this quiet space, I remember the song of a robin, heard from next door's tree, piercing the still morning air with its sad beauty; snowdrops pushing through half-frozen earth to bloom in defiance of the darkness; breaking moist, seedy bread into steaming, home-made stew, savouring the taste; being held in a hug by someone who knows and accepts me.

And so, as dark clouds blot out the sun and rain hammers our dreary garden, this is how I continue to *'choose life'*.

What raises your spirits on cold, dreary days?

15. Snowdrop

I am still confident of this: I will see the goodness of the Lord in the land of the living. Wait for the Lord; be strong and take heart and wait for the Lord. Psalm 27: 13-14

There's nothing in the garden
to cheer my spirits:
no colour, presence,
inspiration.
No gentle snow
to cover dying vegetation,
only crumbs of frost
clinging numbingly
to leaf and post,
clenched in winter's fist.
Yet, as I scuff the frozen earth
a slight green point appears,
thrusting upwards.
A tiny shoot,
defying gloom,
slapped and bullied
by the wind.
Prophet of the spring,
singing
quiet songs of hope
when all around
is desolate and bare.
Why choose to grow and bloom
in darkest winter days
and grace this wilderness
with whispered tales of life?
The spring is not yet come.
We can only wait.

We can only wait

16. Worth more than many sparrows

'Are not two sparrows sold for a penny? Yet not one of them will fall to the ground apart from the will of your Father...So don't be afraid; you are worth more than many sparrows.'
Matthew 10:29-31

There's a flurry of activity as sparrows mob the feeders in our back garden. There are loads of them, living in a colony in and around our prickly hedge, hopping amongst the thorny stems, constantly cheeping as they stand guard on the topmost branches, our own Neighbourhood Watch. Of course they are terrible bullies, intimidating the sensitive goldfinches and smaller tits, but you can't help loving them.

Over the last few years, the RSPB Big Gardenwatch has confirmed that, despite gradually declining numbers, the house sparrow is still the most observed bird in our gardens. It seems to owe its wide distribution throughout Europe to its ability to live in communal groups closely associated with people, even utilising our left-overs.

'Consider the birds...' says Jesus in Matthew 6.

In Jesus' day, you could buy two sparrows for the equivalent of a penny. They were regarded by the Jews as an acceptable food source - though it's hard to imagine finding much meat on a sparrow! Nevertheless, Jesus holds these insignificant creatures before us saying that each tiny life, each unnoticed death is known and valued by its Creator (Matt.10:29). He goes on to say that we too, who are 'worth more than many sparrows' are also tenderly regarded by God. Whether we are ambitious opportunists or bedraggled outsiders, God our Father looks on each one with understanding and delight.

As I watch the birds through the kitchen window, revelling in the counterpoint of their collective song, I know that as soon as I open the back door they will take flight. Wild and timid, they can only be observed, fed and known from a distance. Perhaps this is God's dilemma as he looks on our world, longing to get up close and personal but sensing our fear, our resistance, our disbelief.

Long ago, God came amongst us, as one of us. He came through Jesus Christ to show us the way of compassion, forgiveness and new life.

With a little courage, we <u>can</u> make our own still space for this God to come closer. As we grow in trust, we may even begin to discover that we are beloved, that we are *'worth more than many sparrows'*.

Neighbourhood Watch!

17. Peace Lily

Lord, make me an instrument of your peace: where there is hatred, let me sow love; where there is injury, pardon; where there is doubt, faith; where there is despair, hope; where there is darkness, light; where there is sadness, joy.
Prayer attributed to St. Francis of Assisi

I opened the door into our dining room. There on the windowsill was a small plant I had recently brought in from the greenhouse. But what on earth had happened to it? The leaves had collapsed into a limp heap. Guiltily, I examined the pot and found it quite dry. I dashed to the kitchen for water and carefully moistened the soil, wondering if my neglect had caused any permanent damage.

The plant was a Peace Lily, from the genus *spathiphyllum*, known for its upright, glossy green leaves and white flowers, or *spathes*. Originally a stunning, tropical plant, it thrives in moist, shady corners of conservatories but has also become a popular houseplant, flowering in spring and summer.

The Peace Lily is said to create an atmosphere of beauty, purity and serenity, calming emotions and promoting happiness but as I looked at my little, floppy plant, I was reminded that bringing peace is a costly business. It's not about looking calm and serene but about being peace-makers in difficult situations; mediating in places of conflict; giving, helping, forgiving. If we wish to follow the famous words attributed to St. Francis of Assisi and become channels or instruments of God's peace, we must be willing to pay the price – as Jesus did on the cross.

To do this we must look beyond ourselves, our own strength and abilities, and draw on God's resources, coming back constantly to God in prayer, being fortified by his Word, and guided by the Holy Spirit. We need to keep our 'soil' moist each day, receiving God's water of life. Without this we will begin to droop and fail.

It was a few hours later when I came back to my Peace Lily. I found it strong and vibrant, its leaves firm and pointing upwards. Just a little water had brought about this transformation. Perhaps the secrets of life and even of resurrection are written into God's Creation if we have eyes to see.

Come Holy Spirit.
Pour upon us your life-giving water.
When we are stressed or discouraged, refresh us.
When we are empty and yearning, fill us.
Make us channels of your peace to a broken world.
Amen.

18. Spring Flowers

'See! The winter is past; the rains are over and gone. Flowers appear on the earth; the season of singing has come.'
Song of Songs 2:11-12

Pushing through cold earth,
gentle snowdrops defiantly
proclaim the spring.

Daffodils laugh
at ever-changing skies of grey,
choosing life.

Deep-scented bluebells,
sheltering in silent retreat,
breathe life's mystery.

Softly-shaded blossom,
etching bright blue skies,
scents the heavens.

Irresistible spring progress
urges us to put our trust
in resurrection.

I love daffodils, they give such hope and joy.
What are your favourite spring flowers?

19. The daffodil

'Fear not, for I have redeemed you; I have called you by name; you are mine.' Isaiah 43: 1

I can't help feeling excited in the weeks leading-up to Mothering Sunday when roadsides and gardens, supermarkets and florists are brightened with an abundance of daffodils, splashing intimations of Easter amongst the restraints of Lent.

As a student, many years ago, there was nothing I liked better than to buy bunches of daffodils to take home as

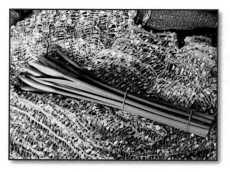

a gift for my mother for there is something magical about the transformation of those sickly-looking, green sticks into the extravagant yellow trumpets of spring.

Back in the early 1980's, I was considering the next step in my career and feeling very uncertain about what I should do so I asked for prayer at our evening service at church and was profoundly touched by the Holy Spirit. That night, I found myself so full of God's presence that I couldn't sleep. In the midst of all my thanks and wonderings, I believe God gave me a picture, a vision if you like.

I saw myself as a daffodil bud, tightly enclosed in its outer sheath, thin, green, giving little promise of beauty. Seeing it, I was afraid that the bud might not open at all but wither and fail. As I watched, however, the flower began to open. It became a bright, bold bloom with a powerful fragrance. I felt that God was showing me what I could become under his care as the Gardener.

A short time later, I heard that, back at home, one of my mother's friends had been praying for me. Quite independently, she was given a picture of a daffodil.

I have held onto this 'vision' over many years, through disappointment, ill health and struggle. Sometimes my daffodil has seemed vibrant, sometimes decidedly bedraggled. Gradually, though, I have seen a blossoming in my life and the release of some fragrance. There have also been times of dying back, resting, new growth and flourishing.

I would never describe myself as like a daffodil. Introverted, diffident, awkward, I am more like a tiny, creeping wayside flower, easily overlooked, pale and not terribly impressive. But God sees me differently. He calls me April, child of the spring, blooming through sunshine and showers alike, bringing joy and blessing to those around me.

Well, it's hard to argue with God so I keep trying to hold on to the promise of the daffodil. Perhaps, one day, I will become a perfect flower, at home in God's heavenly garden, growing eternally under his care.

20. Empty Space
A song of Mary Magdalene

'Woman,' he said, 'why are you crying? Who is it you are looking for?' Thinking he was the gardener, she said, 'Sir, if you have carried him away, tell me where you have put him, and I will get him.' Jesus said to her, 'Mary.' John 20: 15-16

There's no one here:
no soldiers, angels, mystery gardeners,
just an empty space,
sunshine sifting into shadow,
a bloodied cloth, neatly folded.

I find it hard to stay away,
haunted by that body
hanging on the cross,
lying limp
in Mother Mary's arms.

And yet these dreadful memories
are scattered by the sunburst
of a brand new day
and Jesus, our Jesus,
alive again.

I've seen him, briefly,
by the tomb,
and yet I miss
those carefree rambles in the hills,
the arguments and laughter.

I lay my flushed face
on the slab
where he lay,
fingering the stain,
feeling tears well up again.

This is a hard, new beginning.

But as I take one last, long look
around the empty tomb,
I hear a voice
in the garden,
amongst the bright, spring flowers:

Jesus,
calling me.

God holds our world in his love

21. In isolation

'I have told you these things, so that in me you may have peace. In this world you will have trouble. But take heart! I have overcome the world.' John 16: 33

The early morning sunshine kissed my cheek as I walked slowly round the garden, drinking-in the fresh colours of the April flowers, the unfurling new leaves, the progress of the frog spawn in the pond. So hard to believe that somewhere, not far away, people were dying from the corona virus that had turned our world upside down. Medics were working flat out; shops shut; churches closed. So hard not to feel a little guilty in our relatively safe isolation.

I was reminded, however, of Mother Julian, the 14th Century mystic who, after recovering from a near fatal illness, chose to spend her days in the isolation of a tiny cell attached to St. Julian's Church in Norwich. Here she spent her time reflecting and writing, ultimately producing her unique theological work, *The Revelations of Divine Love,* the first work written in English by a woman.

Julian's cell had two windows, one looking into the church, through which she received the bread and wine of Holy Communion, one onto the street so that she could counsel those who sought her aid. Within the cell, Julian made her own still space to commune with God and intercede for a world ravaged by disease, violence and poverty while recurrent outbreaks of the Black Death reduced the population of Norwich by half. It was in isolation that Julian discovered and lived out her calling.

I wonder what Julian would say to us today in our turmoil and anxiety as natural disasters rock the planet and climate change shatters our complacency. Perhaps she would offer the same simple encouragements that ring out from *The Revelations*: that God, who made our world, continues to hold it in his love and look after it.

> *He did not say, 'You shall not be tempest-tossed,*
> *you shall not be work-weary,*
> *you shall not be discomforted.'*
> *But he said, 'You shall not be overcome'.*

(quoted from *Enfolded in Love, Daily Readings with Julian of Norwich*, Robert Llewelyn, ed., Darton, Longman & Todd)

Isolation, whether enforced or desired, offers some of us a chance to slow down and appreciate what is around us. We don't actually need church buildings to appreciate God's creation or show love to others, even if we can only communicate by phone, email or via social media. Lockdown has taught us that we can pour out our prayers as we walk the dog, stand in a distanced queue or fix a rainbow in our window.

As we move forwards into an unknown future, let's trust in the One who holds us, who loves us and died for us. In our own still spaces, we can be the people God intends us to be. We can follow Jesus as his disciples and beloved friends and we can learn to live our lives to the full. And we can respond to God's cry in the garden by returning his love.

For, as Julian of Norwich said, we shall not be overcome.

Creator God, we thank you for the wonders of creation. Show us how we can protect and care for the world around us. Amen.

22. Thanks

Give thanks in all circumstances
1 Thessalonians 5: 18

Thanks to God my loving Father,
Thanks for all that you provide,
Thanks for memories, life-affirming,
Thanks for Jesus by my side.
Thanks for springtime's bursting freshness,
Thanks for autumn's rich decline,
Thanks for tears that you weep with me,
Thanks for peace I know is mine.
Thanks for prayers that you have answered,
Thanks for times when you say no,
Thanks for storms that I have weathered,
Thanks for all that makes me grow.
Thanks for pain and thanks for pleasure,
Thanks for comfort in despair,
Thanks for grace that none can measure,
Thanks for love beyond compare.
Thanks for bluebells in the woodland
Thanks for sunshine and for rain,
Thanks for the one who died to save us,
Thanks for freeing us from blame.
Thanks for joy and thanks for sorrow,
Thanks for the Spirit's power in me,
Thanks for hope for each tomorrow,
Now and for eternity.

Inspired by a hymn by August Ludvig Storm of the Swedish Salvation
Army (1891) Transl. Carl E Backstrom, (1931)

To God be the Glory

In memory of my mother
Hazel Lilian Thompson